SNAPSHOTS IN HISTORY

THE BATAAN DEATH MARCH

World War II Prisoners in the Pacific

by Robert Greenberger

THE BATAAN DEATH MARCH

World War II Prisoners in the Pacific

by Robert Greenberger

Content Adviser: Lester Tenney, Ph.D.,
Professor Emeritus, Arizona State University,
Former POW and survivor of the Bataan Death March

Reading Adviser: Katie Van Sluys, Ph.D.,
School of Education, DePaul University

Compass Point Books ✦ Minneapolis, Minnesota

✦ COMPASS POINT BOOKS

151 Good Counsel Drive
P.O. Box 669
Mankato, MN 56002-0669

This book was manufactured with paper containing
at least 10 percent post-consumer waste.

For Compass Point Books
Robert McConnell, XNR Productions, Inc., Catherine Neitge,
Ashlee Suker, LuAnn Ascheman-Adams, and Nick Healy

Produced by White-Thomson Publishing Ltd.
For White-Thomson Publishing
Stephen White-Thomson, Susan Crean, Amy Sparks,
Tinstar Design Ltd., Lester Tenney, Peggy Bresnick Kendler,
and Timothy Griffin

Library of Congress Cataloging-in-Publication Data
Greenberger, Robert.
  The Bataan Death March: World War II prisoners in the Pacific/by
Robert Greenberger.
     p. cm.—(Snapshots in History)
  Includes bibliographical references and index.
  ISBN 978-0-7565-4095-1 (library binding)
  1. Bataan Death March, Philippines, 1942—Juvenile literature.
  2. World War, 1939-1945—Prisoners and prisons, Japanese—Juvenile
literature. 3. Prisoners of war—United States—Juvenile literature.
4. Prisoners of war—Philippines—Juvenile literature. 5. War crime
trials—Juvenile literature. 6. Death march survivors—Juvenile literature.
I. Title. II. Series.
  D767.4.G74 2009
  940.54′725209599—dc22   2008038920

Visit Compass Point Books on the Internet at
www.compasspointbooks.com
or e-mail your request to
custserv@compasspointbooks.com

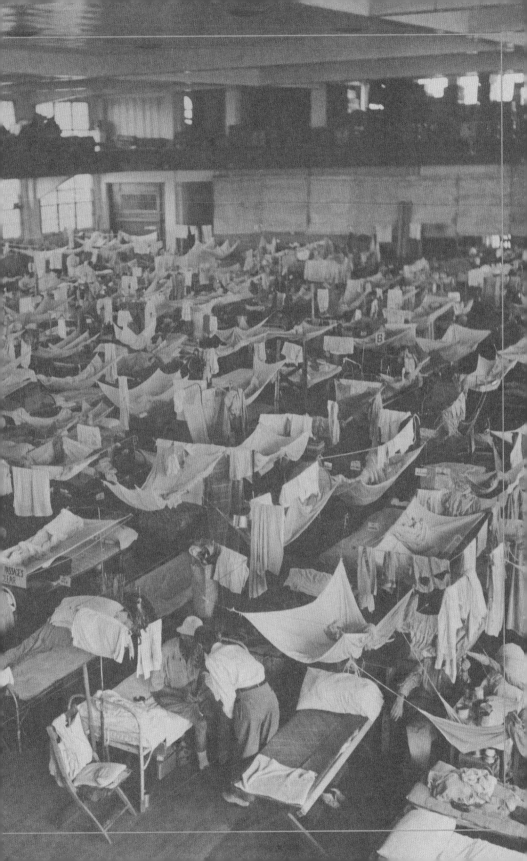

CONTENTS

Walking On 8

The Fall of Bataan 16

The Death March 32

Imprisoned 46

Moving to Cabanatuan............................54

The Great Raid 62

War Crimes Trials 70

The Survivors 78

Timeline..86

On the Web...89

Glossary..90

Source Notes...91

Select Bibliography/Further Reading.......93

Index 94

About the Author/Image Credits 96

Walking On

April 1942 in Bataan, a province in the Philippine Islands, was unbearably hot. The morning sun shone brightly across the islands of the South Pacific and beat down on the dusty ground. Thousands of men slept restlessly, not knowing what was in store for them. For the American and Filipino prisoners of war (POWs) on a forced march to a prison camp, the sun was an unwelcome guest. It signaled the start of another horrific day at the mercy of their Japanese captors.

The POWs were American and Filipino soldiers who had fought to keep Japan from taking control of the Philippines. The Japanese had invaded the islands within hours of their attack on Pearl Harbor, which had brought the United States into World War II.

American troops and their Filipino allies held up their hands in surrender to Japanese forces.

Defeated, exhausted, and ill, around 72,000 American and Filipino soldiers were now the prisoners of the Japanese.

Private Leon Beck, one of the captured Americans, woke up hungry, thirsty, and weak from fatigue caused in part by months of fighting the Japanese on half-rations. Like the thousands of other soldiers on the weeklong march, he slept on bare ground without bedding. There was no mosquito netting to keep the insects away.

Beck and his fellow prisoners were enclosed by barbed wire wound tightly around nearby trees at night. They had no latrine facilities, so the men were forced to foul their sleeping area and try to sleep through the smell. Other prisoners had occupied the same space while passing through the previous day. The sun had baked their waste, which attracted flies and created an overpowering stench.

As the sun beat down, Beck and the other POWs were formed into four columns, each with 25 men. Four to six Japanese soldiers were charged with keeping the POWs moving. Each cluster of men was supposed to be separated from the next by 100 yards (91 meters), but in reality there was no particular order to the thousands of marching prisoners.

The assembled men waited, standing in the increasing heat, until the Japanese gave them the order to resume marching. Beck sweated as he strained to remain in formation, lest one of the guards beat him. Finally, seemingly at whim, a shout went out and the prisoners began to move. For no particular reason, the men were forced to increase their speed, marching double-time. All around Beck, sicker men who could not keep pace fell out of formation and were left behind to die on the hot, dusty road. It quickly became apparent that falling down meant death.

As they marched, the soldiers simply focused on their next footsteps, forgetting thirst, pain, and everything else. When they could no longer carry their meager belongings—helmets, canteens, mess kits, blankets—they dropped them on the side of the road and carried the bare minimum. They stuffed their pockets with lightweight items such as toothbrushes, photographs, or letters from home.

The prisoners of war were usually forced to march in a four-column formation.

11

They did their best to help each other keep the pace. A guard might smack a faltering fellow prisoner with the butt of his rifle or, worse, stab a comrade with the rifle's other end—the bayonet. Two men would walk as close as possible to a weaker third man who shuffled between them. They were trying to hold him upright and keep him moving … and alive.

Allied prisoners used crude stretchers to carry soldiers too ill or weak to walk on their own.

The Japanese soldiers and the Korean guards who were allied with them changed positions regularly and were rotated among the marching groups of soldiers. Guards usually walked alongside

the marching men. A few would walk in front of or behind their prisoners. The captors were also hungry and tired, and they were not prepared to care for so many unexpected prisoners. Beck never knew how particular guards would react. When the columns passed a well, some guards might allow the prisoners to stop and fill their canteens, whereas the guards from the previous day would have kept them marching. Similarly, how the guards reacted to a sick prisoner would vary day to day. Beck described trying to help a prisoner who was in trouble:

> *They wouldn't let you go back and take care of him, even at the artesian [spring] wells, when the prisoners would break and run for the water. They'd shoot indiscriminately into the crowd and some got shot and laid there. You couldn't go take care of them.*

The seriously malnourished and the ill were left to die. The surviving soldiers were too weak to dig graves or do anything else but keep marching.

Alf Larson, a member of the U.S. Army Air Corps, was also among those on the march. His days, like Beck's, blurred together. He watched as local Filipinos tried to toss food to the prisoners. If spotted by the guards, the civilians were beaten or shot to death. They offered such foods as raw sugar or balls of rice, which they shared from their own meager supplies. Larson walked past decomposing bodies of Filipino women lying alongside the bodies of uniformed Filipino and American soldiers.

Japanese and Korean soldiers guarded American POWs captured during the fighting in Bataan.

Although Larson's column of prisoners passed wells filled with cool, clear water, the men were forced to keep moving. They scooped up muddy water from caribou wallows. These were water-filled depressions alongside every road where animals would sit and cool off. Larson described how the prisoners obtained water at night:

> We were not allowed to go to the artesian wells, which were about half a block from the road. We were able to get water at night by collecting canteens. You didn't dare get too many or they would rattle. We would handle them very carefully and quietly sneak off to an artesian well. You held a canteen under water and filled two or three of them. Then we came back and passed them around. If the Japanese had caught us, that would have been it! We would have been shot.

The water gave many prisoners dysentery, an infection of the intestines that gave them diarrhea. Though ill, they were forced to keep marching, soiling their pants as they walked.

Neither Beck nor Larson nor any of the other soldiers were able to keep track of the days. They focused only on survival. If they ate anything at all, it was one or two balls of mushy rice as they marched, with barely any water. The 60-mile (96-kilometer) march took about six days for many men. But for others the experience was twice as long, given the difficulties in moving so many people in the same direction on narrow roads. Larson recalled how he managed to survive the ordeal:

Once the march started, everything just sort of froze in my mind. I was pretty numb the whole time. I didn't think and I didn't feel. I was like a robot and just kept moving. Other than daylight or dark, I lost all track of time. I had to blank everything out and focus straight ahead. I lived from day to day, in fact, hour by hour. The only thing I thought about was the moment and, the good Lord willing, I'll get through the day.

Finally, Larson, Beck, and the thousands of other survivors like them stopped marching. They were then packed into railroad freight cars for the final few miles to their destination, Camp O'Donnell. ◣

The Fall of Bataan

Chapter

2

In the late 1930s, as war tensions spread across Europe, Japan sought to take control of Asia. Japan wanted to control the entire Pacific Ocean and all countries touching its waters. After occupying mainland China, Japan turned to the Philippines, in the southwest Pacific Ocean. By capturing these strategic islands, the Japanese would extend their influence. They could use the Philippines as a base from which to launch attacks against the West Coast of the United States.

On December 7, 1941, Japan launched aerial assaults on American military bases in the Philippines and the American naval base at Pearl Harbor in Hawaii. The next day, the United States declared war on Japan and entered World War II. In the days that followed, Japan intensified its assault on the Philippines.

American naval yards in the Philippines burned following a Japanese attack on December 10, 1941.

American General Douglas MacArthur, who had retired from the U.S. Army, was in charge of the weak army of the Philippines. He had taken the post at the invitation of the Philippine government. But with no real sense of the impending danger, MacArthur was lax in his preparation for war. He required little more from his troops than long hikes and drilling with weaponry. When the war came, the Filipino forces were combined with American troops. Later they became part of the combined Allied forces that included Great Britain, France, the Soviet Union, and the United States.

Two-Sided Global War

During World War II, which lasted from 1939 until 1945, battles were fought in Europe, northern Africa, the Middle East, southeast Asia, China, and the Pacific Ocean. When the war started in Europe in September 1939, Japan sought to align itself with the European powers of Germany and Italy.

In September 1940, representatives of the three countries signed the Tripartite Pact in Berlin, Germany. It formally sealed their wartime alliance as the Rome-Berlin-Tokyo Axis. The pact meant that any country declaring war on Japan, Germany, or Italy would in essence be declaring war against all three Axis powers.

The next year, Japan attacked American military bases in the Philippines and at Pearl Harbor in Hawaii. In response, the United States entered the global war. The United States, Great Britain, France, the Soviet Union, and other countries were known as the Allies. Thousands upon thousands of young Americans enlisted in the military, and others were drafted. All were hastily trained and sent to either Europe or the Pacific.

Immediately after their aerial attacks on U.S. military bases, Japanese ground forces under the command of General Masaharu Homma began invading the Philippines. The troops advanced quickly. By December 12, 1941, there were 2,500 Japanese soldiers on the island of Luzon, a mere 150 miles (240 km) from the combined American and Filipino forces. The Japanese soldiers were highly disciplined, and they strictly followed the orders of their superiors—no matter how demanding. This gave them an uncontested edge in the coming months.

Alf Larson, an American soldier who had been stationed in the Philippines before the war, described what it was like for Filipino soldiers who served under MacArthur at that time:

> There were nine or 10 different dialects in the various Philippine regions. Soldiers were organized with no consideration as to who came from where. They couldn't even converse! It would be like taking a Chinese soldier and putting him in with an American and neither could speak each other's language.

Representatives of Germany, Italy, and Japan toasted the creation of the Tripartite Pact.

19

MacArthur split the U.S. troops in the region into four commands. He gave Lieutenant General Jonathan Wainwright IV responsibility for the units based on the Bataan Peninsula and near Manila Bay. Wainwright's men were poorly equipped, however. In the years after World War I, the United States had done little to upgrade supplies such as uniforms and guns. So when war broke out, soldiers were poorly prepared to wage a global conflict. It would be another year before American factories started making newly designed munitions, tanks, aircraft, seagoing vessels, and vehicles in large enough numbers to make an impact on the war, either in Europe or the Pacific.

Just before Christmas 1941, more than 43,000 Japanese soldiers landed at Lingayen Gulf on Luzon. Wainwright's forces were poorly prepared. The Japanese troops formed a pincer, two flanks that moved close to one another, like the claw of

DOUGLAS MACARTHUR

In 1903, Douglas MacArthur graduated first in his class at the U.S. Military Academy and was commissioned a second lieutenant in the Army Corps of Engineers. After fighting in World War I, MacArthur served at West Point. Beginning in 1922, he served eight years in the Philippines. President Herbert Hoover then named him Army chief of staff, a post MacArthur held until 1935. In 1937, he retired from the service and accepted an invitation from the Philippine government to become field marshal of its army. At the outset of American involvement in World War II, MacArthur was recalled to duty, promoted and assigned as supreme commander of Allied forces in the southwest Pacific area, adding the Australian forces to his command.

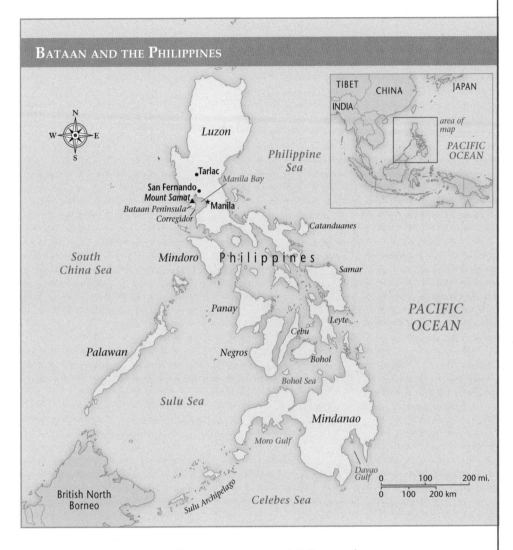

BATAAN AND THE PHILIPPINES

a crab closing. The American and Filipino forces were squeezed back toward Bataan. They had no choice but to give ground to the invaders.

MacArthur and Manuel L. Quezon, the president of the Philippines, were among those retreating to Bataan on Christmas Eve. On December 26, when MacArthur saw that his men could no

American troops retreated to the Bataan Peninsula in late December 1941.

21

THE BATAAN DEATH MARCH

On December 9, 1941, the commander of the Japanese army, General Masaharu Homma (left), arrived with the first wave of Japanese troops on the island of Luzon.

longer sustain a defense, he activated an old military plan called War Plan Orange-3. It called for the soldiers and the government of the Philippines to move to Bataan Peninsula and the island of Corregidor, where they could concentrate their

defensive positions. In theory, this would force the enemy to change tactics and would buy time for U.S. reinforcements and fresh supplies to arrive. The flaw in the plan, though, was that the American Navy was not strong enough in number to challenge the Japanese warships and bring in the much-needed supplies. MacArthur also unwisely ordered that 10 million bushels of food— enough to feed his troops for a year but heavy and difficult to move—be abandoned during the retreat.

THE PHILIPPINES

The islands together known as the Philippines, in the South Pacific, came under the control of the United States as a result of the Spanish-American War in 1898. An independence movement was active until 1935, when the Philippines became a commonwealth. Its steps toward self-governance were interrupted by the outbreak of World War II. Bataan was being used at that time by the United States to store vast amounts of gasoline for its military vessels.

The retreat of men and equipment took several days, from December 30 until January 6, 1942. Japanese troops captured Manila on January 2. With American and Filipino forces isolated on the Bataan Peninsula and Corregidor Island, General Homma's men quickly gained control of the Philippines.

The Japanese, who were better trained than the Allied troops and ready to fight in jungles, used stealth and surprise attacks to find weaknesses in the line. On January 15, the Japanese gained an advantage by going through a gap in troop positions roughly in the center of the Bataan Peninsula. The Japanese forces staged nightly raids and placed Wainwright's men in an impossible position, forcing them to retreat.

As the American troops regrouped, the Japanese pressed their advantage through a new gap until American units closed the hole and stopped the invaders. The back-and-forth fighting that ensued for the next month exhausted the island's defenders and emboldened its attackers. Each side could claim areas of victory and places of defeat, but neither had a clear advantage. The situation, however, was about to change.

General Douglas MacArthur (right), commander of the Allied forces in the southwest Pacific, met with Lieutenant General Jonathan Wainwright in the Philippines.

On February 23, President Franklin D. Roosevelt told General MacArthur that no immediate help would be coming to the Pacific. The American and Filipino solders were going to be hungry for weeks, if not months. In January, the daily ration had provided

> **DAILY RATIONS OF AN AVERAGE U.S. SOLDIER**
>
> - 8.5 ounces (238 grams) of rice
> - 1.5 ounces (42 g) of flour and salt
> - Just over 1 ounce (28 g) of canned meat and canned milk
> - Half an ounce (14 g) of sugar

about 2,000 calories a day. But after January, bread was no longer available. In February, each soldier's daily calorie intake declined to 1,500, and in March, it fell to 1,000 calories a day, a quarter of what was necessary to sustain the average soldier. So starved were the troops that they began eating ponies, mules, iguanas, or monkeys, when they could find them. Soldiers, like many American adults at the time, tended to be heavy smokers, but there were so few cigarettes that they had, on average, fewer than one a day.

The men also had to contend with uniforms and footwear that wore out after weeks without change in the increasingly hot and damp weather. At least a quarter of the men wound up fighting in torn boots, and without rain gear. Things were very different for the enemy. There was a constant stream of fresh Japanese troops and supplies arriving in Bataan by ship, and Homma's troops were backed by artillery.

It soon became obvious that the Allied forces were in trouble. On March 12, President Roosevelt, realizing he couldn't support MacArthur's men, ordered the general to leave Bataan for Australia. The president did not want to lose his commander. MacArthur left with his immediate staff and family. As he abandoned his troops, he uttered the famous line "I shall return." The American and Filipino troops were left to fight the Battle of Bataan with no way to support or evacuate them.

Wainwright was now in charge of all Philippine defenses. He was deeply concerned about the lack of food, water, ammunition, clothing, and basic supplies needed by the American and Filipino troops. Now numbering more than 80,000, they were renamed the United States Forces in the Philippines.

On April 3, Wainwright's fears became reality when 100 Japanese aircraft dropped bombs and fired shells for six straight hours. With Mount Samat, a mountain on the Bataan Peninsula, now a smoking mass of dirt, imperial forces attacked the Allies' left flank. The Allied forces fell back. The unprotected mountain was soon taken by the Japanese, cutting the Allied line in two. U.S. defenses crumbled as the Allied forces struggled to hold ground and then had to retreat during the following days.

On April 6, Major General Edward King, who had replaced Wainwright in the field, ordered a counterattack. But his soldiers were too weak. In

addition to hunger, diseases such as dysentery and malaria had taken hold of the troops. The next day, U.S. gunboats attempted a rescue mission, but they turned back when they saw how badly the Japanese outnumbered them.

Seeing the futility of the situation, King displayed a white flag of truce and asked to meet with the Japanese command. King spoke with Major General Kameichiro Nagano, commanding officer of the Japanese infantry group fighting in the field.

General Wainwright, who was in charge of Allied forces in the Philippines, discussed strategy with his officers.

27

He then met Colonel Motoo Nakayama, Nagano's superior, at a farmhouse near Lamao shortly after 11 A.M. on April 9, 1942. At first Nakayama thought General King was General Wainwright, the superior officer, and he refused to accept surrender from a lesser officer. Nakayama was ready to refuse the surrender and continue the fight, and an argument ensued over the surrender. He then decided to accept King's personal surrender, eliminating the need to discuss terms for all the soldiers involved.

Major General Edward King (second from left) discussed terms of surrender with Japanese officers.

King was prepared to turn himself over to the Japanese, but he first asked Nakayama whether the Allied troops would be well treated. "We are not barbarians," Nakayama told King. With only that assurance, King surrendered. His captors asked for King's sword, but he did not have it with him, so he persuaded the Japanese to accept his pistol instead.

There were around 75,000 American and Filipino forces in the Philippines, considerably more than the enemy's 40,000 men, but the U.S. forces did not have the food and ammunition they needed to fight. The only available troops in the region were on the nearby island of Corregidor with Wainwright, who was shocked to hear of King's surrender. Wainwright telegraphed MacArthur:

MAJOR GENERAL EDWARD KING

Edward Postell King was born in Atlanta, Georgia. He was the grandson of Confederate soldiers in the Civil War. After college, he enlisted in the Army and saw action during World War I. In 1940, King was dispatched to the Philippines, where he served under General Douglas MacArthur. On March 11, 1942, after MacArthur retreated to Australia, King was appointed commanding general of the Philippine-American forces on the Bataan Peninsula. Following his surrender, King remained in Japanese captivity and was repeatedly interrogated and mistreated for more than three years. After he was freed, he was awarded the Distinguished Service Cross for his work in the Pacific. When the war ended, he retired in Georgia, where he died in 1958.

At six o'clock this morning (9 April 1942), General King, … without my knowledge or approval, sent a flag of truce to the Japanese commander. … Enemy on the east had enveloped both flanks. … Physical exhaustion and sickness due to a long period of insufficient food is the real cause of this terrible disaster.

29

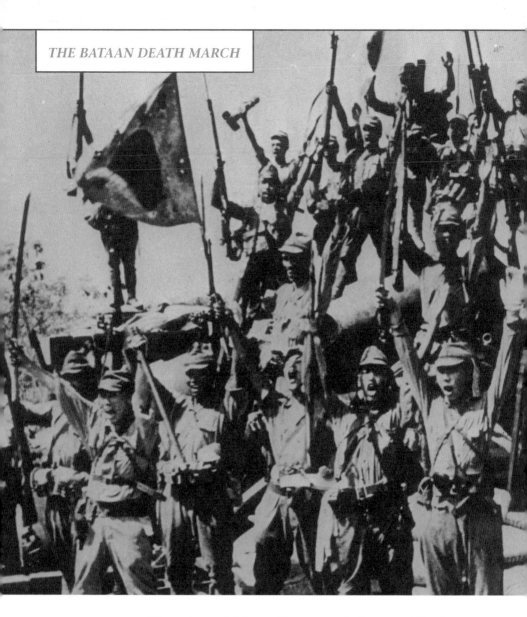

Japanese troops celebrated the capture of an American gun in Bataan.

Homma and his staff suspected that an Allied surrender would come soon, and they had discussed the matter in general terms. But they did not know how many troops would be surrendering. Homma ordered a transportation officer, Major General Yoshitake Kawane, to make arrangements for receiving the Allied prisoners of war. Kawane was given 10 days to figure out what to do with

the troops. He estimated there were 40,000, which was far from the reality. He based his plans on this inaccurate number, which meant that, for the newly surrendered soldiers, the worst was yet to come.

The Death March

Chapter

3

The Japanese men under the command of General Homma were faced with handling around 72,000 prisoners, nearly twice as many as they had anticipated. Complicating matters further, Homma was committed to attacking the Allied command forces on the island of Corregidor, which was two miles (3.2 km) away. He needed the bulk of his troops for this assault on the final American stronghold in the Philippines and felt he could spare no more men for guard duty.

The surrendered U.S. troops were to be marched out of the Bataan Peninsula and northeast 60 miles (96 km) to the city of San Fernando. There they would be taken by rail six miles (9.6 km) to Camp O'Donnell, a former American military base that would serve as

a prison. Despite the overwhelming number of prisoners, Homma insisted that the march begin.

Accounts differ regarding how many men surrendered and were forced to endure the Death March. The constant bombardment from December 1941 until the surrender on April 9, 1942, meant that recordkeeping was difficult. Filipino soldiers

In the harsh sun, Allied prisoners briefly rested on the march to Camp O'Donnell.

33

were not as carefully recorded on duty rosters as were their American counterparts, and when defeat seemed inevitable, many of them shed their uniforms and blended into the native population. That meant they might be listed as missing or presumed dead.

At the beginning of the final battle, General King's command was numbered at 78,000, with 12,000 counted as Americans. The most common estimates are that 62,000 Filipino and 10,000 American men started the march. Upon arrival at Camp O'Donnell, there were perhaps 54,000 walking survivors. An estimated 5,000 to 10,000 Filipino soldiers and 650 Americans died during the march, and another 1,500 or more Americans died at the camp. Many died from the effects of the march. Other deaths occurred in the months that followed as more prisoners were sent to other camps in Japan and the Philippines. The Japanese troops suffered as well. In the months before the Allied surrender, their losses were 2,700 dead and 4,000 wounded. An estimated 13,000 became ill.

Estimated Allied POW Deaths			
	Started the March	Died on the March	Died in the Camps
Americans	10,000	650	1,500–3,000
Filipinos	62,000	5,000–10,000	20,000–25,000

When the march began, the American and Filipino soldiers were in very poor condition. They had been malnourished for months at the time of surrender, and most were suffering from disease. The logistics of moving the men by foot, then by rail, were not carefully thought out. It was simply the wrong decision to try to do so.

Clusters of Allied prisoners walked slowly along the route of the march.

35

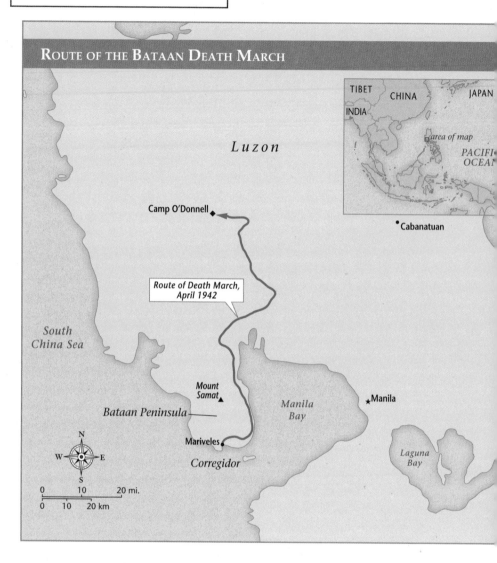

ROUTE OF THE BATAAN DEATH MARCH

Luzon

TIBET CHINA JAPAN

INDIA

area of map

PACIFIC OCEAN

Camp O'Donnell

Cabanatuan

Route of Death March,
April 1942

South
China Sea

Mount
Samat

Manila
Bay

Manila

Bataan Peninsula

N
W E
S

Mariveles

Corregidor

Laguna
Bay

0   10   20 mi.
0   10   20 km

It took most POWs six days to complete the march.

Assisting the Japanese soldiers were conscripts from Korea. Japanese leaders believed in their racial superiority to the Koreans and would not allow them to fight on the front lines on Corregidor, so they were assigned to guard the prisoners. Many of the Koreans resented being given the lesser responsibility, and they took out their frustrations on the prisoners.

As the defeated Americans and Filipinos were gathered in preparation for the march, they were ordered to turn over their possessions. Anything of value, from pocket watches to shaving gear, was taken by the Japanese for souvenirs. American Lieutenant Kermit Lay recalled the procedure used for his group:

> *They pulled us off into a rice paddy and began shaking us down. There [were] about 100 of us so it took time to get to all of us. Everyone had pulled their pockets wrong side out and laid all their things out in front. They were taking jewelry and doing a lot of slapping. I laid out my New Testament. ... After the shakedown, the Japs took an officer and two enlisted men behind a rice stack and shot them. The men who had been next to them said they had Japanese souvenirs and money.*

Word quickly spread among the men to hide or destroy any Japanese money or mementos, because the captors automatically assumed they had been stolen from dead Japanese soldiers.

This was the first time most of the Japanese and U.S. troops had interacted with one another, and neither side was properly trained to understand the other. For example, to the highly disciplined Japanese soldiers, the notion of surrender was unthinkable. They thought the Allied troops should have committed suicide rather than surrender. For that reason, they saw American and Filipino soldiers as unworthy of humane treatment.

The Japanese troops were uncompromising and harsh with their prisoners, who were moved exactly as ordered. The orders made no allowance for the POWs' weakened conditions, the weather, or anything else. Little thought was given to how the ill were to be treated or how the large numbers of soldiers were to be fed.

All the American and Filipino soldiers knew was that they had to march to the trains. So from sunrise to sundown, that is what they did. Nearly all the Japanese showed no mercy. As the blazing sun

beat down on one and all, the Japanese hit the stragglers and the fallen. In some cases, trucks that were passing by ran over the fallen men.

The Japanese treated their prisoners terribly. Every prisoner either personally experienced or saw abuse. Some men were singled out and tortured—not to get military information, but simply for the captors' sadistic pleasure. Later, at the prison camps, some Japanese used torture to learn information, but it was clear that most of the prisoners knew little of value.

A line of American and Filipino prisoners stood under the gaze of a Japanese guard, not knowing what would come next.

On the march, the "sun treatment" was a common form of torture. Prisoners were forced to sit still in the brutal sun, without helmets or other head covering. Anyone who asked for water was shot dead. Some men were told to strip naked or sit within sight of fresh, cool water. Many of the guards delighted in bayoneting or beheading prisoners, treating the soldiers as something less than human.

Allied prisoners sat in the hot sun under the watchful eyes of their Japanese captors.

The American officers expected some kind of dialogue or deference from their Japanese counterparts in recognition of their rank. But they received none. Rank meant little to the

Japanese, who equated one prisoner with another. In addition, because the Japanese troops were often shifted among different groups of marchers, miscommunication was common. To the prisoners, shouting in a foreign language meant little. They couldn't tell whether they were supposed to take a break, march faster, or do something else. The captors focused on a single goal: marching to San Fernando to board the train.

The contempt held by the captors for their charges was shown day after day. One guard would use a bayonet to prod men to stay in line, causing a fresh wound with each poke. Another guard would pour water from a prisoner's canteen into his own canteen and spill the rest on the ground, making the prisoner march under the wilting sun for hours without a drink.

Major Richard M. Gordon, an American Army officer, recalled:

> *First thing I did was receive a good beating. And everything I had in my wallet, in my pockets, was taken from me. And as I was marched down that road where they captured me, I passed my battalion commander, Major James Ivy, and he had been tied to a tree and he was stripped to the waist and he was just covered with bayonet holes. He was dead obviously. And he had bled profusely. He had been bayoneted by many, many bayonets. And that's when I knew we had some troubles on our hands.*

41

While the men were marched along dusty, unpaved roads, they walked through thick, wooded areas, the very same jungle conditions they had fought in. The air was thick with humidity and insects and the sun beat down, so the men easily became dehydrated between stops. Almost every day was hot, bright, and uncomfortable. Whatever rain fell was brief and quickly absorbed into the dirt. Along the 60-mile (96-km) path, they wove through jungles or passed villages, farms, and streams, but rarely were they allowed to linger.

Some Japanese soldiers kept their men moving at a steady clip, while others took their time, since both prisoner and captor were too tired to be able to keep to a schedule. Escaping seemed easy, but there was nowhere to go, and most of the prisoners were too weak or sick to even contemplate surviving on their own in the jungle. Some of the Filipino soldiers, many of whom lived in the vicinity, were able to vanish, but most of them saw the futility in escaping since there was nowhere to seek shelter and avoid recapture.

The dead were left where they fell. There was no time for proper burial rituals or words said over the bodies. Instead, both captors and prisoners saw the fallen not as fellow men but corpses to be picked over. Prisoners took helmets, boots, pants—whatever might replace the torn clothing they were wearing, while the guards grabbed additional souvenirs.

When the prisoners were allowed to stop at wells or streams, they had to line up and get the water in whatever time was permitted to fill their canteens. So that as many prisoners as possible could get water, most of them filled several canteens or just half a canteen, then stepped aside.

Most prisoners, by this time, had one or two others they could rely on. When someone got too sick to walk or keep up, the others carried the man or used their shoulders to prop him up. These buddies would risk their own lives to make

Some prisoners were forced to march with their hands tied behind their backs. Their belongings were strung around their necks.

sure their friends would make it through the day until everyone could rest. The men shared their meager resources. A soldier with a bottle of iodine, which is used to disinfect water, might share some with a prisoner who had packets of dried coffee. Between the two of them, they could use their supplies to treat and flavor the awful-smelling water they found to drink, managing to swallow it and keep moving.

The Japanese—overwhelmed by the number of prisoners— had to divide whatever food they had among 72,000 men. Many of the soldiers recall being fed less than once a day during the march. Cans of food were passed down lines or placed within barbed-wire sleeping enclosures, and the men took turns grabbing handfuls of the mealy rice. At night the men stopped and either were forced to just lie on the ground, with barbed wire set up around them, or were placed in a rice storage building with a metal roof and doors that were locked at night. The following morning, those who had died were left behind.

The night before reaching San Fernando, there was such a great urgency to meet the Japanese schedule that many of the men were marched throughout the night to reach the rail yards in

ACTS OF KINDNESS

During the Bataan Death March, not all Japanese guards were vicious. There are many stories of acts of kindness shown to ailing prisoners. Prisoners were sometimes allowed to care for one another or sneak off for a nap. Some guards secretly gave them tea and crackers. But such accounts of kindness pale in comparison with the tales of abuse.

time. Upon arrival, they were led into small freight cars. The cars were 33 feet (10 m) long, 8 feet (2.4 m) wide, and 7 feet (2 m) tall, and they lacked any sort of ventilation. According to Larson:

> *The train consisted of six or seven World War I-era boxcars. ... They packed us in the cars like sardines, so tight you couldn't sit down. Then they shut the door. If you passed out, you couldn't fall down. If someone had to go to the toilet, you went right there where you were. It was close to summer and the weather was hot and humid, hotter than Billy blazes! We were on the train from early morning until late afternoon without getting out. People died in the railroad cars. I don't know why, but the train stopped at a little town outside Clark Field. They opened the boxcar doors and the Filipinos tried to feed us. The Japanese beat them off with clubs and shut the boxcar doors. The Filipinos tried to throw the food since they couldn't get close to the train. We never got the food. After about an hour, the train started up.*

The march took as little as six days for most, but as many as 12 days for those farthest behind. Of the approximately 72,000 troops who began the march, only about 54,000 walked the final six miles (9.6 km) to their prison home. ◣

Imprisoned

Captain Yoshio Tsuneyoshi was the Japanese officer in charge of Camp O'Donnell, which became a prison for the American and Filipino soldiers. A former U.S. Army training camp designed for 10,000 people, Camp O'Donnell was now expected to house five times that many POWs. The camp was old and poorly maintained. Its condition had been made worse when U.S. forces tried to destroy it as they retreated, in an attempt to deny the Japanese use of the buildings. Now there was one working faucet for the 480 men in eight barracks. Guard towers were hastily constructed, and a mass of barbed-wire fencing ringed the camp.

The prisoners who survived the weeklong march were tired, malnourished, and ill, but their captors had little food and even less medicine to offer. American doctors and other soldiers with medical training took over a barracks and converted it into a hospital, using the medical supplies they had managed to carry with them.

Prisoners at Camp O'Donnell ate small portions of mealy rice.

The Japanese in control of the camp granted the local people permission to give food to the prisoners. It was probably the most food the prisoners had eaten in at least a week, and it was the last time for months that they would eat so well.

At some point during their arrival, the captors told their prisoners that Japan would not abide by the Geneva Conventions. They insisted that the men, now considered "guests" of the Japanese emperor, sign oaths promising that they would not escape. The American commanding officers encouraged their men to sign, assuring them that it would not be held against them. Colonel John E. Olson described the Japanese welcome speech:

> *This was delivered by Captain Tsuneyoshi. ... He let loose with a tirade against the British and Americans for their domination of the Orient [Asia], and asserted that the domination was gone forever. Japan, he said, was now ready to take over the entire East Asia territory. He expressed regret that he was unable to destroy all of us, but the spirit of Bushido [code of honor] forbade such practice. We were assured, however, that the slightest violation of any orders would result in our instant execution.*

The prisoners spent most of their time at Camp O'Donnell standing in line. Because only two water pumps were working, the men had to line up and wait for hours to fill their canteens. The men in line talked of home, favorite foods, or girlfriends—anything to avoid discussing who had died overnight. When they did reach the spigots, they were not always able to fill their canteens to the top, because they were pushed along by other soldiers eager for a turn.

Just beyond the barbed wire ringing the camp was a creek. The American doctors determined that the water there was clean enough to cook prisoners' meager rice rations, but not good enough to drink. Men were assigned by their fellow soldiers to bring water back into camp, and large pots were used to cook rice. It took eight men to carry each 50-gallon (190-liter) drum of water from the creek. Others were assigned by the guards to go outside, under guard, and bring back wood for the fires needed to boil the water. Meat, fruit, and vegetables were nonexistent. What little rice they were given would have to suffice. The morning meal was a watery rice soup called *lugaw* that often contained worms.

THE GENEVA CONVENTIONS

In the 19th century, a group of nations wrote a set of rules, or conventions, for how prisoners of war were to be treated. The first such rules, regarding battlefield casualties, became effective in 1863. After World War I, some nations felt the rules of conduct regarding prisoners needed to be further refined and adopted. Beginning in 1921, national representatives meeting in Geneva, Switzerland, worked for eight years on the new agreement. The major world powers began signing the completed documents in 1929. The United States signed on July 27, 1929. Japan, though, gave only lip service to the accords. Although Japan's representative in Europe signed the document, it was never ratified. As a result, when World War II broke out, the Japanese did not feel bound by the agreement and treated their prisoners as they saw fit. Russia also refused to sign the document. All 194 countries of the world have since signed the Geneva Conventions.

Other assignments made by the prisoners included digging graves and carrying the dead. Each body was wrapped in a blanket slung over a bamboo pole and carried to a mass grave that could hold 20 bodies. The graves were only about 2 feet (60 cm) deep. Bodies were buried naked. The clothing taken from them was boiled and passed on to the living. Some graves were so shallow that the bodies in them were dug up and gnawed at by the camp's dogs.

The Japanese had some prisoners perform specialized work. For example, they asked for mechanics to help them repair damaged vehicles from battle sites and bring them back to the camp. Other POWs were forced to rebuild bridges and repair roads.

Albert J. Senna of the U.S. Army Corps of Engineers, who spent much of his captivity ill and in Zero Ward, the prison hospital, recalled:

PRIME MINISTER TOJO

Hideki Tojo was Japan's prime minister during most of World War II. He had a view toward prisoners that was in line with the longstanding Japanese opinion that people ought to die for their country rather than surrender. He agreed with Japan's not signing the Geneva accords and instructed his guards to be firm. POWs were expected to act like Japanese citizens, with proper manners and respect for their superiors. Given their lack of nutrition and medical care, however, that was impossible. The POWs were considered nonpersons in Japanese eyes for being so cowardly as to surrender. Americans and Filipinos did not think it was cowardly to surrender. Tojo turned a blind eye to the mistreatment of POWs, and he rarely sent anyone to inspect the conditions in which prisoners were kept. He also approved of using prisoners for medical experiments.

They didn't want you to pray, and then, they didn't want you to congregate with a group. They broke them up all the time, because they figured you were up to something, but they were a rough bunch. They killed quite a few guys. They cut off their heads, especially on the March. Anybody give them a rough time, they'd take them out and cut their heads off, but the two guys from my outfit that I know, it was probably illness in camp [that killed them].

At night, men lay down in whatever space in the barracks they could find. They had no bedding and slept on the rough wooden floor. Flies flew about day and night, spreading disease and bothering the men as they tried to sleep.

POWs in Camp O'Donnell tried to cool off in the sparse shade.

51

During the next six months, until sometime in October, nearly 1,500 American soldiers died at Camp O'Donnell, along with as many as 22,000 Filipino prisoners. Those who survived the nights spent much of the days digging mass graves for those who had perished, knowing full well that the following day it might be their turn to be buried.

There were far more prisoners than guards. Due partly to a lack of supervision, approximately 200 American soldiers were able to escape over the first few months. About half of them were recaptured and then beaten. Other escapees died from lack of food or medicine. The first escapees to be recaptured were hung by their thumbs for days as an example to the others.

Most of the guards could not speak English. However, many of them picked up

POW CAMPS IN WORLD WAR II

According to government records, 130,000 Americans were prisoners of war during World War II. In total, about 35 million people were thought to have been POWs at some point during the war. Germany honored the Geneva Conventions with regard to Western prisoners, but those from elsewhere, such as the Soviet Union, were given worse accommodations and treatment. Japan refused to abide by the Geneva protocols. The International Red Cross attempted to get food, supplies and medical materials to the prison camps around the world. In the Pacific theater, though, most packages were confiscated and kept by the Japanese. Prisoners captured by Allied forces were kept in POW camps in many parts of Australia. The Russians alone interned about 3.5 million Axis troops, and at least one-third of them died in conditions that were only slightly less brutal than those in Axis POW camps.

some words and phrases during those months. The Japanese who could speak English were usually assigned to lead prisoner groups away from the camp for the more complicated jobs, such as those requiring engineering skills.

Camp O'Donnell continued to operate as a prison for just under nine months, from April through December 1942. On June 6, the Filipino soldiers were granted amnesty and paroled to their villages. That greatly reduced the number of prisoners left to deal with. In July, Tsuneyoshi was removed from his post as camp commander, and the remaining prisoners were sent to other camps. More than 500 prisoners remained at O'Donnell until its closing. They dug the graves of the 1,500 American POWs who had died, 130 of them from diphtheria, a highly contagious respiratory disease, before the relocation to new camps could even begin. ◣

Moving to Cabanatuan

When General Wainwright surrendered his men at Corregidor on May 6, 1942, they were taken to Cabanatuan City, 100 miles (160 km) north of Manila. There three POW camps—Camps 1, 2, and 3—awaited them.

The three identical camps had originally been U.S. agricultural research stations. Each featured a wooden building divided into offices, a wooden dispensary (medical clinic), a guardhouse with a jail, a garage, and several 60-foot-long (18-m) barracks. Each barracks, designed to house 40 men, brimmed with 120 American prisoners. Across the road from the prisoners' barracks were Japanese guard barracks. Surrounding each camp were 8-foot-tall (2.4-m) barbed-wire fences and several four-story guard towers.

When Bataan was surrendered, the prisoners who were considered too ill to march were immediately transferred to Camp 3. Those who were too ill to move at all were left to die. After Camp O'Donnell was closed, the Japanese again sent the sick prisoners in cramped train cars or by truck to Camp 3.

Japanese soldiers watched as American soldiers surrendered at Corregidor.

55

Conditions at Cabanatuan City, the site of Camps 1, 2, and 3, were superior to those at Camp O'Donnell. The troops at Corregidor had been better fed before their surrender than those at Bataan, and they were stunned to see how ghostly pale their fellow soldiers from Camp O'Donnell looked. The former Camp O'Donnell prisoners were housed at Camp 1. By the end of 1942, about 2,000 prisoners had died in that camp. By comparison, the prisoners housed in Camp 3 were healthier, and records indicate that between June and October only 61 men died there.

In November 1942, the Japanese increased rice rations for all the POWs. In December, packages with food and toiletries from the Red Cross were delivered to the prisoners. Despite the occasional Red Cross deliveries, however, food and other necessities remained sparse and in high demand. Bartering took place among the prisoners and even with civilians and guards. For the sake of survival, people stole from one another or cheated the others out of their rations or supplies. Private Michael Tussing Jr. of the Army Air Corps described getting by:

WAINWRIGHT'S SURRENDER

Deprived of the troops under General King's command, General Wainwright held on at Corregidor, defending the last Allied stronghold in the Pacific, until he had no choice but to also surrender. He gave up on May 6, 1942, one day after the Japanese arrived on the island. Wainwright was held prisoner in Luzon, Formosa, and Manchuria before being freed by the Russian army in August 1945.

General Jonathan Wainwright (far left) surrendered to General Masaharu Homma.

When you made a lot of vinegar, more than you could use, you'd barter for it for something else. Sometimes you'd get someone's rice for a little of your vinegar. By the time we got to Cabanatuan, cigarettes were $100 a pack, if you had the money. ... Money was no good. It was also nonexistent, so everything was barter. Sometimes I could barter or steal raw rice from the kitchen. Then I'd take a round bottle and use it like a rolling pin, and roll the rice so that it was like flour. I'd add water to this and make a batter. Then I'd make pancakes.

At Cabanatuan, the POWs were put to work regularly, often maintaining the grounds or surrounding areas. The daily schedule called for work from 7:30 to 10:30 A.M., followed by a lunch break and then more work from 2 to 5 P.M. Supper took place at 6 P.M., after which the men had free time while daylight lasted, usually until 8:30 or 9 P.M.

Although the rations at the Cabanatuan City camps were better than they had been at Camp O'Donnell, the amount of food remained less than what is considered healthful. Meat was a rare delicacy. For the most part, the men were given rice, mung beans, and sweet potatoes.

The Corregidor survivors and the O'Donnell prisoners were at first wary of one another. The men from Corregidor saw the arriving prisoners as competitors for rations and space, and they were disgusted at their wretched condition. Over time, though, the men all blended together without major incident.

Corporal Charles McMartin was assigned to the hospital section. He later described how the Japanese checked the condition of sick prisoners:

> *During this period, a corpsman [a Japanese army medical man] would come through our hospital barracks once a day, carrying a stick. He walked up and down the aisles looking at the various fellows. If they didn't have their eyes open, he'd hit them real hard on their legs or their side. Some responded, some didn't. When one of them was whacked, he hardly moved. He died a day or two later.*

The survivors said their guards belonged to one of three groups: One was the older regular soldiers who had seen duty in China and were sometimes mean. Another group was the young Japanese soldiers who had never seen battle and tried to prove themselves through cruelty. The third group, the conscripts, had the least esteem of the three and so picked on the POWs.

In late October, 1,000 POWs were sent from the Cabanatuan camps to Dava on the island of Mindanao. Camp 3 was then closed and its prisoners were moved to Camp 1, bringing the total population there to 8,700 men. The lack of proper latrines and sanitation in Camp 1 soon became a problem, although the soldiers crafted a crude sewer system to wash away their waste. This not only kept things cleaner but resulted in less odor and fewer flies.

In December 1942, 300 acres (120 hectares) of land near Camp 1 were dedicated to farming, and 2,000 prisoners were assigned to work the farm in shifts. The farm produced rice, eggplant, okra, corn, radishes, carrots, beans, and peppers. Despite being told it was forbidden, many prisoners smuggled seeds from the farm to create private garden plots at Camp 1.

CIVILIAN POWS

The Japanese occupation of the Philippines was hard for civilian Filipinos. The invading soldiers helped themselves to food and supplies whenever they wished. No money exchanged hands. The Filipino people secretly helped their non-Filipino allies by hiding them or providing them with food. Residents of the Philippines who were from the United States and Europe were taken to Manila's Bayview Hotel or Santo Tomas University. Convents were also places of refuge for international residents. There were about 2,000 American civilians on the islands when the Japanese invaded, and 4,000 international civilians were housed at the university alone. A total of 60 U.S. military nurses were captured, but rather than forcing them to march to Camp O'Donnell, the Japanese relocated them to Santo Tomas University. Civilian POWs were not mistreated, but life remained very difficult for them until liberation came in February 1945.

While conditions at Camp 1 had improved, they were far from ideal. Rule-breaking was punished with beatings, or those involved were stripped and left to lie in the sun for hours, risking dehydration and sunstroke. Early escape attempts were brutally dealt with to discourage others. Five such early

Allied prisoners celebrated Christmas at the Cabanatuan POW camp in 1943.

60

escapees were strung up still alive, hands over their heads, and used by the guards for bayonet practice. Three others were recaptured and forced to dig their own graves at the camp's edge. Then, with the other prisoners watching, the Japanese shot the men, and they tumbled into the ground.

Over time, more American soldiers were sent from the Cabanatuan camps to other POW camps, beginning with 1,000 prisoners sent to Dava. Others went to China, Japan, or Korea to work as slave laborers in mines, farms, and factories. Conditions there were rougher and colder than in the South Pacific, and many weakened men immediately died. The POWs taken to other countries were placed in unmarked ships. The vessels were known as "hell ships" because of the terrible conditions, including the constant risk that the ships would be attacked. ◥

The Great Raid

In 1943, as U.S. industrial might churned out submarines, battleships, tanks, and airplanes, the tide turned against the Japanese. U.S. naval power, coupled with that of the British navy along the Asian coast, put Japan on the defensive. As the Japanese losses mounted, they could not replace men or material as fast as the Allies could.

In October 1944, MacArthur was back in the Philippines and retook Leyte. By December 14, the Allies had recaptured enough islands, and gathered enough ships and men, to consider retaking Luzon. Fearing invasion and the chance that the prisoners would turn on their captors, the guards at a POW camp on Palawan executed about 150 Americans by burning them alive in an air-raid shelter.

As the Allied forces began to retake the Pacific, the Japanese became concerned that the American POWs would be liberated and swell the ranks of the enemy. As a result, the Japanese accelerated their relocation of prisoners to China, Japan, and Korea. From September through December 1944, more and more prisoners were crammed into "hell ships."

In October 1944, General Douglas MacArthur (left) returned to the Philippines.

An American B-25 bomber dropped bombs on a Japanese ship during World War II.

The ships carrying prisoners were unmarked and sailed in convoys mixed with other supply ships, and they were often attacked by American submarines. The submarines were unknowingly killing Americans. By the time the war ended,

5,000 American POWs, more than the death toll at Camp O'Donnell, had been killed by torpedoes or depth charges (underwater explosive devices).

By early 1945, MacArthur was ready to take back the rest of Philippines. On January 9, Allied forces from the United States, Australia, New Zealand, the Netherlands, and the Philippines landed on Luzon and rapidly approached Manila. Until then, American leaders had been largely unaware of what had happened to the POWs. Now intelligence about them began flooding in, and that was when Lieutenant General Walter Krueger, an Australian commander, learned of the Cabanatuan camp.

General Krueger, worried that the Japanese would kill the POWs, decided to rescue them. He assigned the mission to Lieutenant Colonel Henry Mucci and his ranger battalion. On January 27, teams led by First Lieutenants William Nellist and Thomas Roundsville went behind enemy lines to survey Camp 1. They also met with Filipino guerrilla fighters.

Mucci's forces, reinforced by another group of rangers, moved behind enemy lines, staying in the jungle to avoid detection. Just five miles (8 km) from the north side of Camp 1, they met with guerrilla Captain Juan Pajota. He warned them that many Japanese soldiers were present, and he persuaded Mucci to wait a day before proceeding.

On the morning of January 30, Nellist and Private Rufo Vaquilar disguised themselves as Filipinos and went to a shack with a view of the camp. Mucci decided to again split his forces into smaller groups and to send one team to raid the camp while another team provided covering fire. He estimated that the raid would take no more than 30 minutes.

Mucci also called in the U.S. Army Air Corps. One of its P-61 Black Widow night fighter planes flew over the camp. The plane distracted the Japanese guards, letting the rangers safely cross a relatively open, flat field. The pilot repeatedly turned off his engine and restarted it, beginning at a height of 1,500 feet (458 m). Each restart created a loud backfiring sound, and each time the plane dropped about 200 feet (61 m). The pilot flew as low as 30 feet (9.2 m) from the ground, creating the impression that he had a stalled plane. The plane vanished over the hills, making the guards think it may have crashed and distracting them from the sight of men moving on the ground.

Those precious moments allowed the American troops to gain ground. They now were right outside the camp's gates. The rangers began firing their small arms at 7:40 P.M., creating chaos among the Japanese guards. A bazooka team fired at a truck, a squad of Japanese soldiers, and a tin shack that was said to contain tanks. Historian Hampton Sides described what happened next:

At first, the prisoners failed to understand. They were too mentally brittle to process the chaos. Fearing the worst, they took refuge in the barest and most pitiful of hiding places. To one Ranger, who had sliced his way through the fence with wire cutters, the inmates of Cabanatuan looked like "scared vermin scattering for cover after you switch on the kitchen lights." They huddled in corners, cowered in black-water ditches, lurked behind frail bamboo posts, praying for a slimness that even they could not affect. Some were literally scurrying from their deliverers.

Finally the weary and dazed prisoners were led outside to freedom. Other soldiers went to the Zero Ward, the camp's hospital, where the weakest men remained. Some were so malnourished that a single ranger could carry two out at a time.

Freed soldiers walked out of their prison camps in January 1945.

67

Some of the Japanese guards fought hard, but most ran off into the jungle or were killed. Those who fled ran right into the gunsights of guerrillas under Pajota's command. Pajota also saw to it that a bomb destroyed a bridge to keep Japanese tanks from coming to aid the guards.

The Bataan prisoners of war were mostly sickly, many barely alive, when they were liberated in 1945.

A flare signaling the successful rescue, which MacArthur and the other Americans had expected to see hours earlier, finally went up at 8:15 P.M. Mucci had been told that his unit had just captured Talavera, a small town 10 miles (16 km) away. He was directed to bring his troops and the rescued POWs there.

All told, 511 men were rescued from Cabanatuan. Only three died during the operation: a prisoner ill with malaria; battalion surgeon James Fisher, who was wounded by mortar fire; and Corporal Roy Sweezy, who was shot twice in the back during the raid. In contrast, 523 Japanese were counted as dead or wounded.

The fighting in the Pacific dragged out for several more months, but once the Axis powers surrendered in the spring, it was only a matter of time before the war came to a conclusion. The Japanese signaled their surrender in August, formally ending the war in September. ◣

War Crimes Trials

Even though Japan did not sign the 1929 Geneva Conventions, the Allies accused the Japanese of breaking other international laws and even Japanese laws. In September 1945, a month after Japan's surrender, General MacArthur ordered 39 Japanese leaders arrested. Most of them were in Prime Minister Hideki Tojo's Cabinet.

To provide a way to put the accused Japanese on trial, the International Military Tribunal for the Far East, a type of court, was created in Tokyo on January 19, 1946. It operated for three years. A former U.S. assistant attorney general, Joseph Keenan, was made chief prosecutor. He was assigned the high-profile trials involving crimes against peace. An Australian, Sir William Webb, was named the tribunal's president. The court

Joseph Keenan and General Douglas MacArthur met at Allied headquarters in occupied Tokyo.

heard its first case on May 3, 1946. The tribunal investigated the war crimes of those involved in the Bataan Death March and Japanese POW camps.

The accused were put into one of three categories: Class A (for crimes against peace), Class B (for more conventional war crimes), or Class C (for crimes against humanity). Of the accused, 25 were given Class A status and were tried in Tokyo, while 5,700 others were charged with Class B or Class C crimes and were tried elsewhere.

LIEUTENANT GENERAL MASAHARU HOMMA

Masaharu Homma was born on Japan's Sado Island in 1888 and graduated from the Imperial Japanese Army Academy in 1907. Homma spent eight years as a diplomat in England, and he fought with the British Expeditionary Force during World War I. He grew to understand Western culture and was posted to the United Kingdom from 1930 to 1932. Homma returned to field duty in 1933 as a Japanese army commander and was later sent to conquer the Philippines. He insisted that his troops treat the natives as friends, not prisoners, and took an enlightened view toward Filipinos and Allied troops. His superiors overruled his actions, and he was forced to take a harsher approach than he would have preferred. Once Corregidor fell in May 1942, Homma was politically maneuvered aside. He was forced into retirement in August 1943. After the war, Homma was arrested and sent to stand trial by an American military tribunal instead of the International Military Tribunal for the Far East. He was considered by many to be solely responsible for the Bataan Death March, and he was found guilty of committing war crimes. General MacArthur ignored the pleas of Homma's wife, and Homma was executed by a firing squad on April 3, 1946.

When the trials ended, 984 of the accused war criminals were convicted and sentenced to death, although 64 were not executed. A total of 475 were given life sentences, and another 2,944 received shorter prison terms. Only 1,018 men were found to be not guilty, and 279 were never formally accused. Between 1946 and 1951, a total of about 5,600 accused Japanese stood trial, with some 2,200 cases heard outside Japan.

Among those executed were Japanese Prime Minister Hideki Tojo, General Masaharu Homma, and Lieutenant General Tomoyuki Yamashita. Tojo and Yamashita, among others, were hanged at Japan's Sugamo prison on December 23, 1948.

Japanese General Tomoyuki Yamashita arrived at his war crimes trial and was found guilty.

General MacArthur spared Emperor Hirohito and the imperial family from standing trial in order to offer some continuity of Japanese leadership and as a sign of compassion. Critics said that because the imperial family avoided trial, the defeated Japanese people had trouble accepting their connection with the horrible acts committed by their country during the war.

Japan was harshly criticized for its poor treatment of POWs. Among the charges were accusations that the Japanese had subjected prisoners to experiments ranging from testing biological weapons on them

Japanese Emperor Hirohito, who did not stand trial after the war, met with General MacArthur in September 1945.

to injecting them with animal blood and surgery without anesthesia. One gruesome experiment involved frostbite—a prisoner was left exposed to subfreezing temperatures and then doused with water, literally freezing his arms and legs. When a limb was frozen, it was cut off for testing. Some American, European, Russian, and Chinese POWs were reduced to having only a head and torso—and were then subjected to further testing. One description of the germ experiments came from Hiroshi Matsumoto, a former Japanese medic:

> *There were seven cages in each of several rooms. The cages were only big enough for one naked Chinese to sit cross-legged. Unit members injected the prisoners with a variety of bacteria and observed them for three or four months. Blood samples were then taken from the prisoners and they were killed. The cages were seldom empty.*

MacArthur exempted Japanese scientists from charges in exchange for being given the results of their biological warfare research. Because of that exemption, the full extent of the atrocities was referred to only once during the trials.

For an example of how atrocities were dealt with at the trials, 23 people were found guilty of vivisection—wrongful removal of body parts. Five were sentenced to death, four to life imprisonment, and the rest to shorter terms, all of which were shortened two years later.

During the war crimes trials, 28 military leaders were brought before the International Military Tribunal for the Far East in Tokyo.

Japan's brutal treatment was not limited to POWs. Other victims included women in the lands occupied by Japan. More than 200,000 women from these countries were forced into prostitution. They were called "comfort women," and they were kept near Japanese military bases. Imperial military forces coerced women to work in China, Indochina, and Indonesia. At the time of the trials, much of the women's testimony was kept from the public, and only in recent decades has the extent of the crimes become clear. The Japanese government was forced to provide compensation to the surviving women.

The issue of compensation has haunted the Japanese government since the war ended. The Potsdam Declaration, which the Allies used to dictate the terms of Japan's surrender, called for money to be given to victims of war crimes. Japan eventually agreed, paying more than $9 million through the International Red Cross to victims around the world. Despite these efforts, some Asian governments never gave the money to the people affected. Other claims, notably those from China, which had been brutally invaded, were abandoned.

The Treaty of San Francisco, which formally ended the war with Japan, was signed on September 8, 1951, by 48 nations and Japan. The treaty's text did not confirm the legality of the International Military Tribunal for the Far East. Japanese law did not, and still does not, consider the men convicted of war crimes to be criminals. This policy made it impossible for those convicted to appeal their cases. Japan spent decades negotiating over restitution with the countries it occupied and damaged. In today's dollars, Japan paid more than $1 billion in compensation between the end of World War II and 1976, when the final payment was made to the Philippines. ◣

The Survivors

O nce they were freed, the sickest POWs were sent to makeshift recovery areas in the Philippines. Others were sent back to the United States, to military hospitals there. Their physical ailments were treated. What went untreated were the long-term problems caused by years of malnutrition and diseases. Medical science did not know then how to treat such conditions.

Most of the former prisoners didn't have high hopes for their future. Albert J. Senna, a surviving veteran, later said:

> *A lot of them gave up on the trip [back home], because they said we wouldn't be welcomed home, which we weren't. You know, they covered everything up. I mean, they never did come out with the truth, all the tortures and heads cutting off and all that stuff.*

Former American POWs were moved to a Santo Tomas University gym in the capital of the Philippines after being released from a Japanese prison.

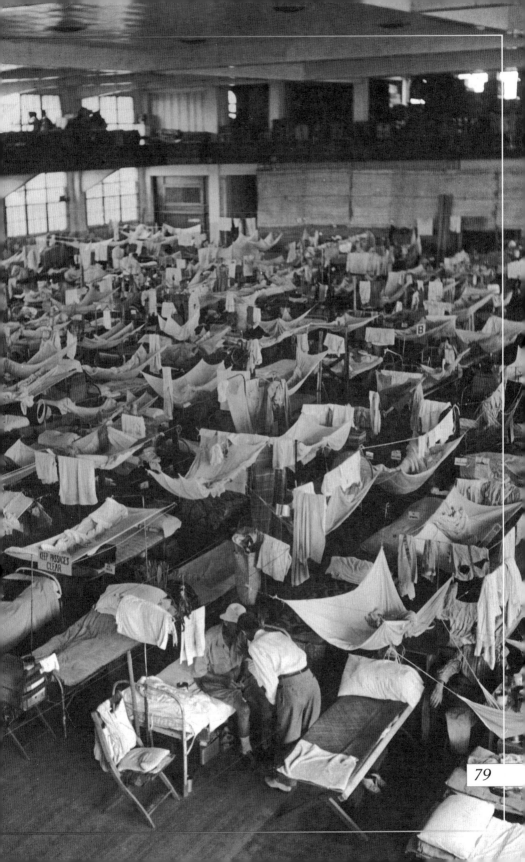

After the war, more than 3,500 American graves were found around Camp O'Donnell.

The psychological toll of the men's experiences was hardly considered. The field of psychiatry was in its infancy. "Post traumatic stress disorder," which is commonly diagnosed today in survivors

of horrific experiences, wasn't recognized as a legitimate condition until the Vietnam War, which took place more than 20 years after World War II.

Some military officials estimate that one-third of the former POWs died within a year of returning to the United States—some from lingering disease, others from suicide. The soldiers who continued to live had higher rates of suicide and alcoholism than other World War II veterans. Ruben Flores, an Army cook, later recalled:

> *I don't think there's anybody that will ever forget what we went through. I don't care how happy you are, you come back to it. You might have a good time all night and tomorrow you go back to thinking to what you went through.*

Most of the survivors returned to their homes and families, left the military, and re-entered the work force. The vast majority of former POWs rarely spoke of what they saw and endured during the war. More than a half century later, the historian Hampton Sides wrote:

> *The men of Bataan are famous for their iron reticence. They're stoics. Seldom in our history has such a large group of men endured so much and complained so little. Many of them never told their stories when they returned home, not even to their own families. For many of the POWs, it has taken 50 years to sift their experience and begin to make sense of it.*

Americans at home had heard of the Bataan Death March, but the full extent was not understood until *Death March*, an oral history that was compiled by Donald Knox, was published in 1981. Since then, more former POWs have come forward to share their stories. Many wrote memoirs, surviving children wrote about their parents, and today accounts are numerous.

Fewer than 1,000 survivors of the Bataan Death March are still alive now. But in recent years, the survivors have tried to preserve the memory of their ordeal. In 2001, the Battling Bastards of Bataan was formed as a clearinghouse of memories and information. The survivors track down information, correct inaccuracies in the news media, and organize reunions of former POWs. The group takes its name from a poem written by Frank Hewlett, a prisoner during their incarceration. Hewlett wrote the poem in 1942:

GENERAL JONATHAN WAINWRIGHT

Jonathan Mayhew Wainwright IV graduated from the U.S. Military Academy in 1906 and saw action in France during World War I. After the war, he was part of the occupying forces in Germany until 1920. Wainwright continued to be promoted until he was a brigadier general in command of the 1st Cavalry Regiment at Fort Clark, Texas, at the dawn of World War II. After the war, he returned to the Philippines to accept the surrender of the local Japanese commander, Lieutenant General Tomoyuki Yamashita. Wainwright was promoted to four-star general and given the Medal of Honor for his efforts on Corregidor. He remained in the Army until his retirement in 1947. He died in 1953 and was buried at Arlington National Cemetery.

We're the Battling Bastards of Bataan,
No mama, no papa, no Uncle Sam,
No aunts, no uncles, no cousins, no nieces,
No pills, no planes, no artillery pieces,
And nobody gives a damn!

Two Filipino World War II veterans visited the War Heroes Cemetery at the Philippine army headquarters during Veterans Week.

A MEMORIAL MARCH

As more people learned of the sacrifices these men made in the Philippines, events to formally remember them were organized. In 1989, the Army ROTC unit at New Mexico State University started a memorial march. The march grew in popularity, and in 1992 White Sands Missile Range and the New Mexico National Guard signed on as co-sponsors. Only 100 people marched the first year, but the march has since grown to include 4,000 people, including civilians who walk alongside the men in uniform. Members of families attend the marches to honor the memories of their fathers, brothers, or other people connected to them.

The United States has paid tribute to this special group of men with the names of bridges in New Mexico and Chicago, and stretches of highway in Indiana and New Mexico. Memorials to them have begun appearing around the United States, and there are several annual re-enactments of the events that help raise money for soldier care or other memorials. An 8-foot-tall (2.4-m) bronze statue, *Heroes of Bataan,* stands in Las Cruces, New Mexico. It is the only federally financed memorial for the Bataan Death March in the United States, and it is fittingly located in the state that lost the most men during the Philippines portion of the war.

In 2008, Representative Tom Udall of New Mexico introduced congressional legislation to award all participants in the Bataan Death March the Congressional Gold Medal. He suggested that a single medal be crafted and placed in the Smithsonian Institution to honor the soldiers.

Virgilio Gonzalez, a Filipino survivor of the Bataan Death March, and his wife, Caridad Gonzalez, reviewed names of his comrades at the Capas National Shrine, where the prison camps once stood.

The Philippines remembers the roughly 72,000 soldiers who were taken prisoner in 1942 with memorials at Camp O'Donnell, Mount Samat, and elsewhere. At Mount Samat are the 310-foot-high (95-meter) Memorial Cross and the Shrine of Valor. April 9, the day King surrendered to the Japanese, is now called *Araw ng Kagitingan* (Day of Valor), a day of remembrance in the Philippines. ◗

Timeline

September 27, 1940

Japan signs the Tripartite Pact with Germany and Italy, forming the Axis alliance.

December 7, 1941

Japan attacks Pearl Harbor.

December 8, 1941

Japan attacks Clark Field in the Philippine Islands. The United States declares war on Japan and enters World War II.

December 10, 1941

Japan dispatches soldiers to the Philippines. By December 12 about 2,500 Japanese soldiers are on Luzon, 150 miles (240 km) from U.S. forces.

December 26, 1941

General Douglas MacArthur activates War Plan Orange-3, which consolidates U.S. forces on Bataan and Corregidor.

January 2, 1942

Japanese soldiers occupy Manila, the capital of the Philippines.

February 23, 1942

President Franklin D. Roosevelt notifies McArthur that no immediate help is coming to the Pacific region.

March 12, 1942

Roosevelt orders MacArthur to go to Australia.

April 3, 1942

Japan launches its final offensive on Bataan.

April 6, 1942

Major General Edward King orders a counterattack, only to be informed that the soldiers are too weak to do so.

April 9, 1942

King surrenders 72,000 soldiers at Bataan to the Japanese.

April 10, 1942

The march begins. Thousands of American and Filipino POWs die during the next 10 days.

April 16–19, 1942

POWs who survive the march are interned at Camp O'Donnell.

May 6, 1942

General Jonathan Wainwright surrenders Corregidor.

June 6, 1942

Filipino POWs are paroled from Camp O'Donnell.

October 1, 1942

The first "hell ship" leaves the Philippines, taking POWs to camps elsewhere in the Pacific.

December 1942

Land near Cabanatuan's Camp 1 is dedicated to farming, and 2,000 American POWs tend the fields.

October 20, 1944

MacArthur returns to the Philippines.

December 14, 1944

Nearly 150 Americans are executed by their Japanese captors in a POW camp in Palawan.

January 27, 1945

General Walter Krueger sends Lieutenant Colonel Henry Mucci and his rangers to raid Cabanatuan and liberate remaining POWs.

January 29, 1945

The rangers meet with guerrilla Captain Juan Pajota at Balincarin. Mucci postpones the raid for 24 hours.

January 30, 1945

11:30 A.M.

The raid at Cabanatuan begins. Lieutenant Bill Nellist and Private Rufo Vaquilar, in disguise, gain access to an abandoned shack above the camp and prepare a detailed report on camp activities.

2:30 P.M.

Mucci receives the Nellist report.

3 P.M.

Captain Robert Prince gives his plan for the rescue mission to Mucci.

6:50 P.M.

A P-61 Black Widow plane distracts the prison guards. Rangers gain positions, and a firefight ensues.

7:40 P.M.

The evacuation begins.

7:45 P.M.

Juan Pajota and his guerrilla unit hold off suicidal Japanese forces, securing the rangers' positions.

8:15 P.M.

A flare signals that the assault and rescue are over.

February 11, 1945

Former POWs leave the Philippines for the United States.

August 14, 1945

President Harry Truman announces the end of the war with Japan.

Timeline

September 2, 1945

Japanese General Tomoyuki Yamashita surrenders the Philippines; Japan formally surrenders.

January 19, 1946

 The International Military Tribunal for the Far East is created in Tokyo, Japan.

February 11, 1946

Japanese generals Masaharu Homma and Tomoyuki Yamashita are found guilty of crimes of war in American tribunals.

April 3, 1946

Homma is executed by firing squad.

May 3, 1946

 The International Military Tribunal for the Far East hears its first case.

December 23, 1948

Seven Japanese convicted of war crimes by the International Military Tribunal for the Far East are executed at Sugamo Prison in Tokyo.

ON THE WEB

For more information on this topic, use FactHound.

1 Go to *www.facthound.com*
2 Choose your grade level.
3 Begin your search.
This book's ID number is 9780756540951
FactHound will find the best sites for you.

HISTORIC SITES

Bataan Memorial Military Museum and Library
1050 Old Pecos Trail
Santa Fe, NM 87505
505/474-1670

This learning center was started by veterans shortly after World War II.
It focuses on troops sent to the Philippines.

The Bataan-Corregidor Memorial
Kissimmee, Florida
407/846-6131

This memorial of a scene from the Bataan Death March features an American
soldier, a Filipino soldier, and a Filipino woman.

LOOK FOR MORE BOOKS IN THIS SERIES

1963 Birmingham Church Bombing:
The Ku Klux Klan's History of Terror

Dred Scott v. Sandford:
A Slave's Case for Freedom and Citizenship

Tiananmen Square:
*Massacre Crushes China's
Democracy Movement*

A complete list of **Snapshots in History** titles is available on
our Web site: *www.compasspointbooks.com*

Glossary

Allies
friends or helpers; when capitalized, refers to the United States and its allies during major wars

atrocities
acts that are usually considered monstrous by most societies

barracks
building or buildings used to house soldiers

bayonet
blade attached to the end of a rifle and used as a weapon in close combat

Bushido
Japanese code of honor that demands unquestionable loyalty and obedience and places honor before life

civilians
people not part of a military force

commonwealth
state or nation that rules itself but also maintains ties to a larger nation

conscripts
people forced into military service

Corps of Engineers
branch of the U.S. Army dedicated to civil and military engineering projects, such as bridges and dams

dysentery
disease of the intestines caused by infection and marked by severe diarrhea

malnutrition
condition caused by an unhealthful diet

munitions
materials used to wage war, including ammunition and weapons

peninsula
area of land surrounded almost entirely by water

post-traumatic stress disorder
condition experienced by soldiers or civilians who survive catastrophic events

published
presented to the public in printed form

ratified
formally approved

rations
fixed portions of food, usually in relation to soldiers but sometimes applied to civilians

Red Cross
international philanthropic organization that provides help during times of war or natural disaster

tribunal
court of justice usually associated with the armed forces

Source Notes

Chapter 1

Page 13, line 12: "Capture and Death March." *American Experience*, PBS Online. 30 Jan. 2008. www.pbs.org/wgbh/amex/macarthur/sfeature/bataan_capture.html

Page 14, line 8: Rick Peterson. "Back to Bataan: A Survivor's Story." 2 Feb. 2008. www.bataansurvivor.com

Page 15, line 16: Ibid.

Chapter 2

Page 19, line 17: "Back to Bataan: A Survivor's Story."

Page 29, line 5: "The Bataan Surrender." Battling Bastards of Bataan. 30 Jan. 2008. www.battlingbastardsbataan.com/lamao.htm

Page 29, line 26: Gary J. Wright. "Death March: The Other View." 6 April 1984, GlobalSecurity.org. 26 Feb. 2008. www.globalsecurity.org/military/library/report/1984/WBJ.htm

Chapter 3

Page 37, line 8: Donald Knox. *Death March: The Survivors of Bataan*. New York: Harcourt Brace Jovanovich, 1981, p. 116.

Page 41, line 20: "Capture and Death March."

Page 45, line 5: "Back to Bataan: A Survivor's Story."

Chapter 4

Page 48, line 15: John E. Olson. *O'Donnell: Andersonville of the Pacific*, 1985. 26 Feb. 2008. www.us-japandialogueonpows.org/Olson.htm

Page 51, line 1: "Interview with Albert J. Senna." 17 Oct. 2005. *Rutgers Oral History Archives, New Brunswick History Department*. 22 Feb. 2008. http://oralhistory.rutgers.edu/Interviews/senna_albert.html

Chapter 5

Page 57, line 1: Ibid., p. 212.

Page 58, line 17: *Death March: The Survivors of Bataan*, p. 203.

Chapter 6

Page 67, line 1: Hampton Sides. *Ghost Soldiers*. New York: Doubleday, 2001, p. 274.

Chapter 7

Page 75, line 12: News Watch, 2 Feb. 2008. www.arts.cuhk.edu.hk/Nanjing Massacre/Watch.html

SOURCE NOTES

Chapter 8

Page 78, line 12: "Interview with Albert J. Senna."

Page 81, line 11: Ruben Flores. *Effects after the war. Post 1945 Battle for Bataan.* 30 Jan. 2008. http://reta.nmsu.edu/bataan/timeline/post1945.html

Page 81, line 22: *Ghost Soldiers*, p. 337.

Page 83, line 1: "Back to Bataan: A Survivor's Story."

SELECT BIBLIOGRAPHY

Breuer, William B. *The Great Raid*. Hoboken, N.J.: John Wiley & Sons, 2002.

Knox, Donald. *Death March: The Survivors of Bataan*. New York: Harcourt Brace Jovanovich, 1981.

Petak, Joseph A. *Never Plan for Tomorrow*. Valencia, Calif.: Delta Lithograph Company, 1991.

Sides, Hampton. *Ghost Soldiers*. New York: Doubleday, 1991.

FURTHER READING

Haugen, Brenda. *Douglas MacArthur: America's General*. Minneapolis: Compass Point Books, 2006.

Klam, Julie. *Victory in the Pacific*. North Mankato, Minn.: Smart Apple Media, 2003.

Rice, Earle. *Strategic Battles in the Pacific*. San Diego: Lucent Books, 2000.

Wukovits, John F. *Life as a POW*. San Diego: Lucent Books, 2000.

Index

A

Allied forces, 18, 20, 26, 29, 30, 32, 34, 37, 52, 56, 63, 65, 72, 77
Arlington National Cemetery, 82
Axis powers, 18, 27, 52, 69

B

Bataan Peninsula, 22–23
Battle of Bataan, 26
Battling Bastards of Bataan (organization), 82
Battling Bastards of Bataan (poem), 82–83
Beck, Leon, 10–11, 13, 15
Bushido (code of honor), 48

C

Cabanatuan City, 54, 56, 57, 58, 59, 65, 67, 69
Camp 1, 54, 56, 58, 59–60, 65
Camp 2, 54, 56, 58
Camp 3, 54, 55, 56, 58, 59
Camp O'Donnell, 15, 32–33, 34, 46–53, 56, 58, 59, 65, 85
civilians, 13, 48, 56, 59, 72, 76, 84
Clark Field, 45
communication, 19, 41, 52–53
compensation, 76–77
Congressional Gold Medal, 84
conscripts, 36, 59
Corregidor Island, 22–23, 29, 32, 36, 54, 56, 58, 72, 82

D

daily schedule, 57
Dava, 59, 61
deaths, 11, 13, 34, 41, 42, 45, 49, 50, 51, 52, 53, 55, 56, 62, 64–65, 68, 69, 73, 75, 81
depth charges, 65
diseases, 15, 27, 35, 51, 53, 69, 75, 81

E

escape attempts, 42, 48, 52, 60–61
executions, 48, 62, 72, 73, 75

F

Fisher, James, 69
Flores, Ruben, 81

food, 13, 15, 23, 25, 26, 29, 38, 44, 45, 46, 48, 49, 50, 52, 56, 58, 59
France, 18

G

Geneva Conventions, 48, 49, 50, 52, 70
Germany, 18, 52, 82
Gordon, Richard M., 41
Great Britain, 18, 48, 62
guards, 10–11, 12–13, 32, 36, 40, 41, 42, 44, 46, 49, 50, 52, 54, 56, 58–59, 61, 62, 66, 68

H

health care. *See* medical care.
"hell ships," 61, 63–65
Heroes of Bataan statue, 84
Hewlett, Frank, 82–83
Hideki, Tojo, 50
Hirohito, emperor of Japan, 74
Homma, Masaharu, 19, 23, 25, 30, 32, 33, 72, 73
Hoover, Herbert, 20

I

illnesses, 10, 13, 15, 34, 35, 38, 44, 46, 50, 51, 53, 55, 58, 69, 75, 78, 81
International Military Tribunal for the Far East, 70, 72–73, 77
International Red Cross, 52, 56, 77
Italy, 18
Ivy, James, 41

J

Japan, 8, 16, 18, 19, 34, 48, 49, 52, 61, 62, 63, 70, 73, 74, 76, 77

K

Kawane, Yoshitake, 30–31
Keenan, Joseph, 70
King, Edward "Ned" P., 26, 27–29, 34, 56, 85
Knox, Donald, 82
Korean soldiers, 12, 36
Krueger, Walter, 65

L

Larson, Alf, 13, 14, 15, 19, 45
Lay, Kermit, 37
Leyte, 62
Lingayen Gulf, 20
Luzon Island, 19, 20, 62, 65

M

MacArthur, Douglas, 18, 19, 20, 21–22, 23, 25, 26, 29, 62, 65, 69, 70, 72, 74
Manila, 23, 54, 59, 65
Manila Bay, 20
maps, 21, 36
march participant estimates, 34, 45
march schedule, 32, 42, 44
mass graves, 50, 52, 53, 61
Matsumoto, Hiroshi, 75
McMartin, Charles, 58
medical care, 46–47, 50, 52, 58, 67, 78, 80–81
medical experiments, 50, 74–75
Memorial Cross, 85
memorials, 84–85
Mindanao Island, 59
Mount Samat, 26, 85
Mucci, Henry, 65, 66, 69

N

Nagano, Kameichiro, 27
Nakayama, Motoo, 28, 29
Nellist, William, 65, 66

O

officers, 27, 28, 30, 37, 40, 41, 46, 48
Olson, John E., 48

P

Pajota, Juan, 65, 68
Palawan, 62
Pearl Harbor naval base, 8, 16, 18
personal items, 11, 37, 41
Philippines, 8, 16, 18, 19, 20, 21, 22–23, 26, 29, 32, 34, 59, 62, 65, 72, 77, 78, 82, 84, 85
Potsdam Declaration, 77
prison camps, 8, 10, 15, 32–33, 34, 46–53, 54–56, 58, 59–60, 62, 65, 85

Q

Quezon, Manuel L., 21

R

railroads, 15, 32, 38, 45, 55
rations, 10, 25, 49, 56, 58
Red Cross, 52, 56, 77
rescue missions, 27, 65–69
retreat, 21–22, 23, 26, 29, 46
Rome-Berlin-Tokyo Axis, 18

Roosevelt, Franklin D., 25, 26
Roundsville, Thomas, 65

S

San Fernando, 32, 41
Santo Tomas University, 59
schedule. *See* daily schedule; march schedule.
Senna, Albert J., 50–51, 78
Shrine of Valor, 85
Sides, Hampton, 66–67, 81
Smithsonian Institution, 84
Soviet Union, 18
Spanish-American War, 23
submarine attacks, 64–65
Sugamo prison (Japan), 73
suicides, 81
supplies, 13, 20, 23, 25, 26, 44, 47, 52, 56, 59
surrender, 28, 29, 30, 37, 50, 54, 56, 85
survivors, 15, 34, 58, 81, 82
Sweezy, Roy, 69

T

Talavera, 69
Tarlac, 85
Tojo, Hideki, 70, 73
torture, 39–40, 60, 78
Tsuneyoshi, Yoshio, 46, 48, 53
Tussing, Michael, Jr., 56–57

U

Udall, Tom, 84
United States, 8, 16, 18, 20, 23, 26, 49, 59, 65, 78, 81, 84

V

Vaquilar, Rufo, 66

W

Wainwright, Jonathan Mayhew, IV, 20, 23, 26, 28, 54, 56, 82
war crimes, 72
War Plan Orange-3, 22–23
Webb, Sir William, 70
World War I, 20, 29, 49, 72
World War II, 8, 16, 18, 23, 49, 62, 69, 77

Y

Yamashita, Tomoyuki, 73, 82

Z

Zero Ward, 50, 67

ABOUT THE AUTHOR

Robert Greenberger is a freelance writer and editor who has written many books for young adults on topics ranging from the history of Pakistan to a biography of Lou Gehrig. He additionally writes fiction and nonfiction for adults, including the *Essential Batman Encyclopaedia* and many works set in the *Star Trek* universe. He lives in Connecticut.

IMAGE CREDITS

Corbis **cover** and p. **35**, pp. **2** and **11** and **86**, **17**, **19**, **22**, **28**, **35**, **63**, **64** and **87**, **74**, **80** (Bettman), **55**, **57**, **67 and 87**; Getty Images pp. **6** and **79**, **68** (Carl Mydans/Time Life Pictures), **9** and **86** and **back cover**, **24**, **30-31**, **33** (Keystone), **27** and **back cover** (Hulton Archive), **60** (US Army/Time & Life Pictures), **71** and **88** (Alfred Eisenstaedt/Time & Life Pictures), **76** and **88** (Central Press); Hulton Archive p. **73**; National Archives and Records Administration pp. **5** and **43**, **12**, **14**, **40**, **47**, **51**; Romeo Gacad/AFP pp. **83** and **back cover**, **85**.